Florida Cookbook

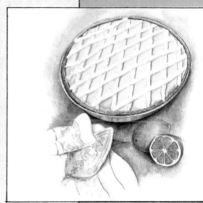

Anne Hardy

**ILLUSTRATED BY
PATRICIA AND
ROBIN De WITT**

First published in 1991 by
The Appletree Press Ltd,
7 James Street South, Belfast BT2 8DL.
Copyright © 1991 The Appletree Press, Ltd.
Illustrations © 1991 Patricia and Robin De Witt used
under Exclusive License to The Appletree Press, Ltd.
Printed in the E.C.. All rights reserved.
No part of this publication may be reproduced or
transmitted in any form or by means, electronic or
mechanical, photocopying, recording or any
information and retrieval system, without permission
in writing from the publisher.

First published in the United States in 1991
by Chronicle Books, 275 Fifth Street
San Francisco, CA 94103

ISBN: 0-8118-0051-2

9 8 7 6 5 4 3 2

Introduction

Florida has an energizing climate, with an average of 220 sunny days a year, and is pleasantly cooled by breezes from both the Atlantic and the Gulf of Mexico. Combined with an average annual rainfall of 53", this magnificent climate yields rich, fat lands on which to farm. When the fruits of the ocean and a cosmopolitan mix of ethnic groups are added, you have a bounty of exotic and delectable foods found nowhere else in North America. Although Florida has one of the highest retiree populations of any state, the food, like the lifestyle, is fun and young. Florida's unique location means that fruits and vegetables normally only available elsewhere in summer are abundant in winter, whilst in summer visitors will find new and unusual produce which has migrated from the nearby subtropics of the West Indies and South and Central America. Many varieties of fish and shellfish are indigenous to Florida, but some are only seasonal. While a fresh catch is economical as well as enjoyable, a selection of frozen and imported fish can be found year round. Florida produces beef cattle (ranking among the nation's top 10 producers), sugar, eggs, honey, pecans, and peanuts. What follows is a sampler of recipes reflecting the choices of cuisine available in a southern state, so near to the Caribbean and Latin America, and influenced by those cultures.

A note on measures
Spoon and dry cup measurements are level. Seasonings can of course be adjusted to taste. Recipes are for four unless otherwise indicated.

Florida Breakfast

There are so many items which could be selected for a typical Florida breakfast, but citrus fruit is always included. Florida's humid climate produces many varieties of juice oranges. Citrus groves abound and bonded fruit shippers are happy to send orders worldwide. The state also produces more than 70 percent of the world's grapefruit crop. It is one of the few places in the country where you can walk into your backyard and pick a fresh grapefruit or orange from a tree. There is nothing like freshly squeezed Florida orange juice to start the day. Valencia, Hamlin and Pineapple are the important juicy varieties.

---

freshly squeezed Florida orange juice
(Valencia, Hamlin or Pineapple varieties)
½ Florida grapefruit (sweeter pink or yellow)
Cuban Toast
Café con Leche (coffee with milk)

Light and airy but crisp Cuban loaves make delicious toast, spread with butter or guava jam. Cuban bread ranks as one of the great contributions made by the Cubans who settled in Florida. The long loaves are thinner-crusted than French bread but much the same.

Cuban coffee is similar to espresso, but usually Colombian coffee is used — Cafe Bustello is a popular local brand. Small, inexpensive Cuban percolators can be found in local stores but you can make Café con Leche satisfactorily in your own percolator. Make the coffee and add an equal amount of boiled milk. More often than not sugar will have been added when the coffee is served in cafés and restaurants.

Crusty Cuban Bread

6 ½ cups (approx) enriched,
all-purpose, (plain) unsifted flour
2 pkgs dry yeast
2 cups water
2 tbsps sugar
2 tsps salt
yellow cornmeal

To make 3 loaves, stir together 2 cups of flour and yeast in the large bowl of an electric mixer. Heat water, sugar and salt, stirring until warm (120–130°F). Add to flour-yeast mixture, beat for about 3 minutes at high speed until smooth. Stir in enough of remaining flour to make a stiff dough. Turn out onto a lightly floured surface. Knead 12–15 minutes until dough is bouncy and elastic and springs back to the touch of your fingers. Cover dough with a large bowl and leave for 45 minutes. Meanwhile grease a baking sheet and sprinkle lightly with cornmeal. Divide dough into thirds and with a rolling pin, roll each third into a rectangle about 10 x 13 inches. Start from the wide side and with your hands roll each piece forward and backwards, pressing the dough into the roll at each turn. Press the ends together to seal and then fold them slightly under the loaf. Place seam side down on the baking sheet. Make small diagonal cuts across the top of each loaf and brush all over with water. Let rise in a warm place (80–85°F) until doubled; about 20 minutes. Put the loaves in a cold oven (do not preheat) and then adjust to 400°F. Bake 40–45 minutes. If they are browning too quickly, cover lightly with foil. Cool before cutting.

Mango Jam

Florida leads the nation in the production of oranges, grapefruit, tangerines, watermelon, green peppers and cucumbers, and is a major source for corn and celery during many months of the year. Less familiar but nevertheless intriguing fruits and vegetables are also grown here. A luscious fruit, which can be as small as a plum or up to 2–3 lbs in weight, is the mango. This fruit has a long flat seed, yellow-red skin, and a golden flesh when ripe .

Select 4 firm-to-ripe mangos and cut into small pieces. Mix with $3/4$ cup sugar to 1 cup mango. Let mixture stand for a few hours until sugar dissolves, stirring occasionally. Cook until thickish. Put in sterilized jars and seal. Delicious and different!

Florida Grouper Chowder

Grouper is the red snapper, or *mahimahi*, found in the waters of Florida's coast. If it is not available then haddock can be substituted.

1/4 lb salt pork (fatback) or 3 strips bacon
2 large onions, sliced
2 potatoes, diced
2lbs skinned and boned grouper
3 cups water
I cup clam/clamato juice
I cup heavy cream
salt and pepper to taste

In a large saucepan, cook salt pork until crisp and brown. Remove and keep. Add onions to fat and cook slowly until just turning golden. Add fish, water, clam juice, potatoes and seasoning. Cook slowly about 30 minutes until fish is tender. If necessary, break up fish into bite-size pieces. Add cream, sprinkle salt pork croutons on top, and serve with crackers.

Egg Lime Soup

Limes are plentiful in Florida — from the small yellow key limes to the larger cultivated green limes found in the supermarkets and at roadside stands. A gift of fresh limes from a neighbor's tree is always wonderful.

---

2 tbsps butter
1 cup chopped sweet onion
$1/2$ cup chopped celery
1 cup grated carrot
6 cups chicken stock
salt and pepper to taste
1 tbsp chopped fresh parsley or $1^1/2$ tsp dried parsley
1 tbsp chopped fresh dill or $1^1/2$ tsp dried dill
3 egg yolks
1 tbsp cornstarch
1 cup milk
$1/4$ cup lime juice

In a large pot or heavy pan melt the butter and add the onion and celery. Sauté for 5 minutes. Add the carrot, stock, seasonings, and herbs. Bring to a boil, lower heat and simmer for 20 minutes. In a blender, combine egg yolks, cornstarch, milk, and lime juice. Blend until very smooth. Add 1 cup of the hot soup stock to the egg sauce and combine thoroughly. Then pour the egg mixture into the pot, stir the soup and gently reheat before serving. Do not boil.

Poorman's Shrimp (Prawn) Cocktail

Since shellfish are becoming scarce and sometimes expensive, this "poorman's" recipe uses less shrimp or prawns than usual. The shellfish comes mostly from the Gulf of Mexico and in many varieties and sizes. To cook $1\frac{1}{2}$ lbs shrimp, boil 1 quart water and 1 tbsp salt, turn down the heat and simmer 2–4 minutes, depending on size. The shell can be removed before or after cooking.

---

6 oz cooked baby shrimp (prawns), peeled, deveined

Salad	Dressing
2 apples	juice of 1 lemon
2 sticks celery	1 tbsp oil
$\frac{1}{2}$ cucumber	3 tbsps salad dressing
1 medium-size avocado	or mayonnaise
pineapple pieces	1 squeeze of tomato
grapes	purée or ketchup
lettuce	

Mix all dressing ingredients until blended. Slice or chop all salad ingredients except for lettuce. Add prawns and sufficient dressing. Mix. Shred lettuce to make a bed for the mixture. Thousand Island dressing is very similar to this homemade one.

Avocado Sorbet

Native to the American subtropics, the avocado is now found in warm climates throughout the world. Many gardens in south Florida have avocado trees and there are dozens of varieties. Known locally as "alligator pears", they can be bought at bargain prices by shopping at roadside stands or buying directly from growers. Avocado sorbet is a simple and delicious way to use up ripe avocados, either as a starter or a dessert.

---

3 large or 4 small ripe avocados
$1/2$ cucumber
3 tbsps confectioners' sugar
3 tbsps lime or lemon juice
fresh mint (or similar herb) to decorate
lettuce

Peel avocados thinly, ensuring that you keep all the flesh, especially the dark green under the skin. Chop the cucumber finely. Put all ingredients in food processor or liquidizer and blend thoroughly. Check flavoring. Freeze. Remove from freezer at least one hour before serving. Serve on a bed of lettuce in cold wine glasses with a sprig of mint on top.

Greek Salad

The Greek population, who live mainly in Tarpon Springs on the Gulf coast north of Tampa, have influenced menus throughout the state. Greek salad is offered widely in restaurants. You can buy domestic feta cheese in most supermarkets, but imported Greek feta has the authentic tang, if you can find it.

10–12 small plum tomatoes
1/2 lb feta cheese
2–3 cucumbers
salt and pepper to taste
2 small onions
1 green pepper
olives

Wash and cut tomatoes into bite-size pieces. Cut cucumbers coarsely and mince onions and pepper. Cut feta cheese into cubes. Put all ingredients in salad bowl and add olives. Season and toss well. Serve with oil and vinegar dressing.

Crab Salad

Two kinds of crab are harvested from Florida waters: the blue or soft-shell crab and the stone crab. Live crabs are cooked in boiling salted water for 20–30 minutes or until they become orange. The best meat is extracted from the large segments of the claws, legs and tail section.

---

2 heads lettuce
1 lb white crabmeat
juice of 1 lemon
1 tbsp olive oil
3 hard-boiled eggs, chopped
dash of cayenne pepper
$1/2$ tsp salt
mayonnaise

Sprinkle crabmeat with cayenne pepper, salt and lemon juice. Add oil and chill until quite cold. Cut $1/2$ head of lettuce in small pieces and mix with crabmeat. Place each serving on a lettuce leaf. Garnish with mayonnaise and chopped eggs.

EL LOI

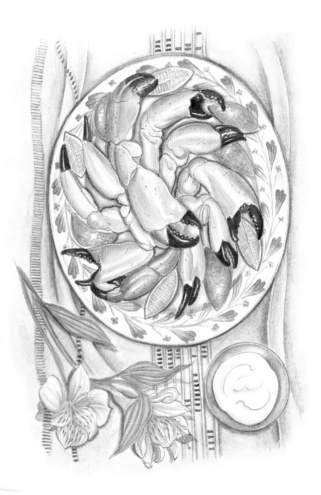

Joe's Stone Crab Mustard Sauce

The stone crab season opens October 15 and ends May 15 as does Joe's restaurant, a landmark on Miami Beach for 78 years. The purplish-red stone crab, considered by some to be the ambrosia of the sea, has become an expensive delicacy worldwide. Crabbers use a long-handled pole with a wire hook on the end to coax the crabs from rocks near beaches, then break off the large claw and return the crab to the water, according to Florida laws. Stone crab claws can be steamed or boiled and are usually served cold in the shell. Crack the shells with a hammer and pick out the sweet, lobster-like meat. Also serve with Key limes or lemons and drawn (melted) butter.

---

3 1/2 tsps dry English mustard
1 cup mayonnaise
2 tsps Worcestershire sauce
1 tsp A-1 steak sauce
1/8 cup light (single) cream
1/8 tsp salt

Blend mustard and mayonnaise and beat for one minute. Add remaining ingredients and beat until mixture reaches a creamy consistency.

Fisherman's Fish

This is a simple but delicious way in which any local fisherman might cook his fresh catch — yellowtail, dolphin (the flat fish, not the mammal!), grouper, or even cod.

---

4 fillets of fish, boned
oil or butter
salt and pepper to taste
1 or 2 limes or lemons

Coat bottom of frying pan with oil or butter and heat gently to medium heat. Season fish with salt and pepper and your favorite spices. Cut limes into quarters and squeeze juice onto fish in pan, spread limes around pan. Cook 3–5 minutes on each side. Skin is easier to peel off after cooking. Serve with parsley potatoes or rice.

Curried Shrimp, West Indian Style

There is a strong West Indian influence in South Florida and dishes from the West Indies are often on local menus. Local ethnic shops sell Jamaican hot sauces, curry powders, and spices.

---

1 medium onion, chopped
1 cup coconut milk
1 clove garlic, crushed
1/2 tsp salt
1/4 tsp white pepper
1/4 cup melted butter
2 lbs uncooked shrimp, peeled and deveined
2 tsps curry powder
1 green mango, peeled and cubed
2 tbsps lime juice
hot cooked rice

In a large skillet melt butter and sauté onion and garlic. Add curry powder and mango, stirring well. Cook about 5 minutes over low heat. Add lime juice, coconut milk, salt and pepper and cook about 10 minutes. Add shrimp to sauce, cook about 10–15 minutes or until shrimp is done, stirring occasionally. Serve over rice.

Florida Lobster

Florida lobster is a spiny lobster, also known as crawfish or rock lobster. Like oranges and grapefruit, once considered a delicacy typifying Florida cooking, it has become rare and expensive. The tail is meaty and there is some meat in the large segments of the legs but it does not have the large front claws or pincers of the lobster from the cold northern waters. Its spine-covered legs and body give it protection. In season, Florida lobsters (or their tails) are offered in restaurants and some markets, usually already boiled and then refrigerated. To cook a live lobster, immerse it head first in boiling, salted water, boil again and continue until it turns red. Split the lobster by placing it on its back and cutting it in half.

---

2 lobsters, boiled and split
I tbsp melted butter
$1/4$ tsp salt
$1/8$ tsp paprika
$1/8$ tsp pepper
Tabasco (hot) sauce

Brush the exposed meat with butter, sprinkle with salt, pepper, and paprika. Add 2–3 drops of Tabasco to each, if desired. Place lobsters about 4" from heat under broiler and cook until the meat turns a very light brown. Serve with melted butter (add a little lime juice and garlic to the butter for extra flavor).

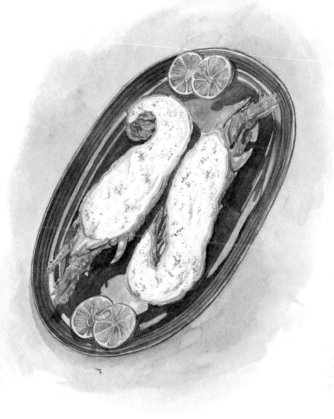

Red Seafood Cocktail Sauce

Sauces for seafood often consist of various mixtures of ketchup with lime juice and seasoning. The following mix is a basic guide, but you can experiment with ingredients until you find the taste you like.

$^1/_2$ cup ketchup
1 tbsp finely chopped onion
1 tsp Worcestershire sauce
2 tbsps horseradish
2 tbsps lime juice
$^1/_2$ tsp soy sauce
2 tbsp finely chopped celery (or 1 tsp celery salt)

Mix all ingredients thoroughly together and chill well. Serve with any seafood dish that requires a spicy sauce.

Arroz con Pollo

(Chicken and Yellow Rice, Cuban Style)

This dish was introduced by the Cubans who originally came to Key West in the 1830's (and later started the cigar industry in Tampa). Cuban meals are more often than not accompanied by black beans which have their own distinctive flavor. Don't let the list of ingredients put you off this tasty and not so difficult dish.

¼ cup Spanish olive oil	1 tsp chopped parsley
1½ small chickens (3½ lbs total) cut in 6 quarters	1 tsp salt
	¼ tsp hot sauce
1 medium onion and ½ medium green pepper, finely chopped	generous pinch saffron
	3½ cups chicken stock
2 cloves garlic, peeled and minced	2 cups long-grain rice
	1 can tiny, French-style, canned peas, heated
1 large ripe tomato, peeled, seeded and chopped	1 canned pimiento, cut in thin strips
1 tsp fresh lemon juice	parsley sprigs
1 bay leaf	

Heat 2 tbsps oil over moderate heat in heavy, non-iron, 10" frying pan until hot (not smoking). Cook chicken 2 or 3 pieces at a time until pale gold, adding more oil when necessary, then transfer to heavy flame-proof casserole with tight cover. Adjust heat to moderately high. Add onion, green pepper and garlic to hot drippings in pan; cook, stirring until onion turns gold. Stir in tomato, blend and spoon mixture over chicken. Add lemon juice, bay leaf, chopped parsley, salt and hot sauce.

Add saffron to 1 1/4 cups of stock, bring to a boil and simmer 5 minutes. Add to chicken, cover casserole and simmer over low heat until chicken is tender, 15–20 minutes. (Meanwhile preheat oven to 325°F.) Bring remaining stock to a boil and add to chicken, add rice, bring to a boil once more, then cover casserole tightly and transfer to oven. Bake for 20 minutes (until rice is tender and liquid absorbed). Uncover and garnish with peas, pimiento, and parsley sprigs.

Churrasco

This is a very popular Nicaraguan dish, almost more so in South Florida than in its native country. Prior to the 1979 revolution, Cuban businessmen would fly to Managua for the day just to eat this for lunch! The most famous restaurant featuring Churrasco was Los Ranchos, which is now operated in Miami by the same owners. Churrasco is usually accompanied by *gallopinto* — rice with red beans.

---

4 tender fillet steaks, seasoned with salt and pepper

Chimichurri Sauce	**Marinara Sauce**
fresh parsley, chopped	*onion, chopped*
olive oil	*ketchup*
vinegar	*vinegar*
salt and pepper	*salt and pepper*
minced garlic	*sweet red or green pepper, chopped*

Cevollas Encurtidas Sauce

onion and jalapeno peppers, chopped	*oregano*
	dry mustard
white vinegar	*sherry*

There are no specific quantities for the sauces, make them to your own taste. Spread the thin Chimichurri sauce over the steak and broil to your liking. Serve with additional Chimichurri sauce on top and with the two additional sauces on the side. The longer the sauces are allowed to marinate, the better.

Everglades Frogs' Legs

The Everglades, or "Sea of Grass", is a subtropical wilderness of swamps, mangroves, and abundant wildlife. The best way to see some of the rare animals, such as crocodiles, manatees, and bald eagles, is by airboat. Most of the tourist attractions in the national park are run by the original Florida settlers, the Seminole Indians. Frogs' legs, which are a delicacy from the Everglades, vary in size. The smaller ones are quicker to cook and more tender, but legs of any size are delicious.

frogs' legs	milk
seasoned flour	cooking oil
minced parsley	lime or lemon
garlic (optional)	

Soak frogs' legs in milk for 30–60 minutes before cooking. Drain and dry them. Fry large legs as you would fry chicken. Lightly dust the smaller legs with seasoned flour, turn in hot shallow fat until brown, about 6–7 minutes, sprinkle with minced parsley, and serve with lime or lemon segments. To give an even more appetizing flavor, cook a cut clove of garlic in the oil at the same time.

Citrus Hamburgers

Almost every day in Florida is ideal for cooking outdoors and most people have a barbecue grill of some kind. In South Florida, hickory chips from the wood of the Australian pine are often used as an excellent smoke flavoring, either alone or with charcoal briquets.

---

2 lbs ground beef
$1/2$ tsp grated orange peel
I tsp orange juice
$1/2$ tsp salt
I bouillon cube
$1/4$ cup bread crumbs
I tsp lime juice
$1/4$ tsp pepper

Dissolve the bouillon cube in $1/2$ cup of water. Put the ground beef and all other ingredients in a bowl, pour the bouillon over them and mix thoroughly. Form the mixture into hamburgers (there should be enough for 8 – 10) and place on the grill, when the briquets glow hot, about 4" above the coals. Cook for approximately 8 minutes on each side.

Plantation Sauce

This is a rather zesty sauce made from locally grown fruits, typical products of a Florida plantation. It can be used on a variety of dishes, including burgers and fritters.

---

3 tbsps butter
3 tbsps brown sugar
1 fresh mango, diced
1 fresh papaya, diced
3 tbsps pecans, chopped
1 tbsp rum
1 cup water

Melt butter in pan and sauté pecans. Add sugar and stir for 2 minutes. Add mango and papaya and mash everything together to a pulp. Add water and bring to a boil. Then add rum and simmer for 15 minutes. Serve hot with any of the burger or fritter recipes.

Conch Fritters

The conch (pronounced "konk") lives on the sea floor near the coast, often near coral reefs, and is native to the tropical waters of the western North Atlantic from the Equator to the Florida Keys. If you are unable to pluck your own conch fresh from the sea, you can buy the meat fresh or frozen from a good seafood market. Conch fritter batter can be made several days in advance and used when needed, or fried and reheated later.

1 pkg yeast	1 tsp dried thyme
1 cup warm milk	1/2 cup parsley
2 lbs conch, skinned and cleaned	1/4 tsp red pepper flakes
1 large green pepper	1/4 tsp cayenne
2 medium onions	1 tsp salt
1 1/4 cups flour	1/2 tsp fresh ground pepper
1 egg	oil for deep frying

Dissolve yeast in warm milk. Chop conch, onions, and green pepper into 1" pieces. Place conch in bowl of food processor fitted with steel blade. Process for 10 seconds. Add onions, green pepper, milk-yeast mixture, flour, egg, thyme, parsley, red pepper flakes, cayenne, salt, and freshly ground pepper. Process 1 minute. The mixture should be well combined, without large lumps, and of uniform texture (take care not to over-process). Cover fritter batter and allow to rest for 1 hour. Drop batter by tablespoonfuls into 2" of very hot oil and fry until golden brown. Keep warm, uncovered, in the oven. Serve with tartar sauce, Red Cocktail Sauce (see p.31) or Plantation Sauce (see p.40).

Cuban Sandwich

½ loaf Cuban bread (see p. 7)
sliced chicken breast
sliced pork
sliced ham
sausage
Swiss cheese slices
butter
mustard
one dill pickle

Take a hunk of a Cuban loaf, halved horizontally and you have the basis for this Florida classic. The filling consists of thinly sliced chicken, pork, ham, sausage and Swiss cheese. The bread is spread with butter on one side, mustard on the other and dill pickle sliced in between. If bought from a vendor, he or she will usually flatten the sandwich, toasting it lightly in a waffle-like sandwich press. Different from the typical American ham and cheese sandwich, the Cuban Sandwich was first sold at sandwich stops in the streets of Havana. For a variety of Cuban food, visit the Calle Ocho (Eighth Street) Festival in Miami's Little Havana each February.

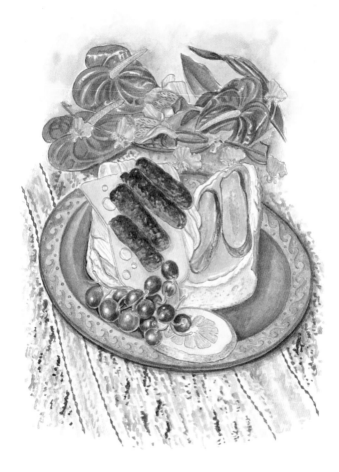

Hush Puppies

One dish you may encounter at a Florida breakfast is a tradition throughout the southeastern US, tasting and looking like its name — grits. Grits are whole kernels of white corn, ground into a coarsely granulated dry form. Some Floridians prefer grits with sugar and milk but the most common way to eat them is hot with melted butter. Many restaurants will offer a choice of grits or home fries with eggs. Cornbread and biscuits are other special culinary masterpieces that bespeak Florida's Old South influences, but when the main dish is fish, hush puppies are the perfect companion. There are numerous ways to make hush puppies but here is a good basic recipe.

---

2 cups cornmeal
1 egg beaten
1 tbsp flour
3 tbsps onion, finely diced
$1/2$ tsp baking soda
1 cup buttermilk
1 tsp salt

Mix all the dry ingredients together, add the egg, onion, and buttermilk. Stir well. Drop $1/2$ tbsp at a time into hot, deep fat. Remove as soon as they float. Above quantities should produce about 1$1/2$ dozen.

Pineapple Salsa

Quick-to-fix salsas are excellent with swordfish, tuna steaks, shrimp, or other fish. Coarsely chopped ingredients offer more texture and are more like salads than sauces. Any berries, tropical or citrus fruits can be substituted for the pineapple in this recipe.

---

1 small fresh pineapple, cut into small cubes
1 small red onion, diced
1 medium red and one medium yellow/orange/purple pepper
(cored, seeded and diced)
$1/2 - 3/4$ tsp finely minced jalapeno or serrano pepper
1 tsp ground cumin
1 tsp ground coriander
2 tbsps lime juice
1 large clove garlic, mashed

It's simple — just combine all ingredients and then serve! If time permits, chill for an hour to allow the flavors to blend. Makes 4–5 cups.

Florida Fried Plantains

Plantains, like other types of bananas, grow in central and south Florida. Peel soft, yellow ripe plantains (the skin comes off just like a banana). Slice crosswise, diagonally to make pieces about 1/4" thick. Fry in hot, shallow fat for about 3–4 minutes on each side. Ripe plantains burn easily so adjust the

heat to brown them evenly. Drain on paper towel, salt to taste and serve hot with pieces of lime or lemon to squeeze on them (and tabasco or Jamaican red pepper sauce for those who like a little hot and spicy flavor). As a vegetable, fried plantains are delicious with ham or chicken. Or, serve them for dessert with a mixture of sugar and cinnamon instead of salt.

Key Lime Pie

The famous Florida dessert, Key Lime Pie, originated in Key West. This recipe will make an authentic yellow pie. If you don't have key limes, use the ordinary kind. Digestive cookies can be substituted for graham crackers.

Pie crust	Filling
1 cup graham cracker crumbs	3 egg yolks
5 tbsps melted butter	1/4 cup sugar
2 tbsps granulated sugar	1/2 cup lime juice
	1 can sweetened condensed milk

Combine cracker crumbs, butter, and sugar, mix well and press firmly into pie dish. Place in freezer (may be prepared a day in advance).

To make the filling, fill a medium saucepan halfway with water and bring to a boil. Combine egg yolks, sugar, and lime juice in a medium stainless steel bowl. Mix with a wire whisk until well combined. Place bowl over boiling water and whisk constantly until frothy and thick. Remove bowl and mix in condensed milk. Pour into pie shell and chill for at least 2 hours.

Coconut Cream Pie

Coconuts grow by the roadside and in many backyards. They are also easily bought at supermarkets or roadside stalls. In "Little Havana", Miami's Cuban district, they are sold green as well as ripe. By chiselling a hole into a cold green coconut and taking a straw, you can drink the clear, refreshing coconut milk right there. The Cubans call this "Coco Frio".

---

1 cup sugar
3 tbsps cornstarch
$1/_8$ tsp salt
2 cups milk
3 egg yolks
1 large coconut, meat grated
$3/_4$ tsp vanilla
1 x 9 inch pie shell
$1/_2$ cup whipping cream

Mix the sugar, cornstarch and salt. Heat milk to almost boiling and slowly add dry ingredients, stirring until mixture is smooth. Cook in a double boiler, stirring frequently. Let cool until lukewarm, then add egg yolks and $1/_3$ of the coconut. Return to double boiler and cook until the mixture thickens. Cool, stirring in the vanilla. Pour into pie shell. Whip the cream and spread over the custard in the shell. Sprinkle remaining coconut over the top.

Melon Bowl

Florida produces virtually all of the various kinds of melons, turning winter into summer for northern visitors and leading the nation in watermelon production. Cantaloupes, honeydews, watermelons and a variety of squash are available to be eaten fresh or made into pies and desserts. The recipe which follows makes an attractive dessert for a buffet.

$1/2$ watermelon
sliced fresh papaya or mango
$1/2$ cantaloupe
I can sliced pears
cherries

Scoop out a half-watermelon, cut the flesh into cubes and remove the seeds. Cut a thin slice of peel from the bottom of the shell so it will stand firmly. Reserve the shell and, if possible, freeze it until it is rigid for easier handling. Combine the cubes of watermelon with other fresh, canned or frozen fruits, varied in shape and color. Allow approximately I cup per serving. Use the syrup from canned fruit as a sauce (or use a little coca cola and fruit juice), and perhaps flavor it with rum, brandy, or bourbon. Cover the bowl and refrigerate until thoroughly chilled. Serve the fruit in the watermelon shell and garnish with fresh mint or scoops of sherbet.

Piña Colada

A visit to Florida would not be complete without a Piña Colada — typical, tropical, cool, and refreshing. Rum is traditionally the "island" liquor, because its origin is sugar cane, grown on most of the Caribbean islands and in Florida. It mixes well with all the tropical fruit juices.

1 scoop cracked/crushed ice
1 oz coconut cream
3 oz pineapple juice
2 1/4 oz white rum
ice cubes
pineapple spear
cherry
jumbo straw!

Combine cracked ice, coconut cream, pineapple juice and rum in a blender and blend well. Pour into a hurricane (tall, lantern-shape) glass and fill with ice cubes. Decorate with pineapple spear and cherry and serve with jumbo straw.

Florida Sunrise

A major crop in Florida, strawberries are grown mostly in the central part of the state, specifically near Plant City. Prime strawberry season is March and April and you can pick your own berries at a bargain rate.

---

6 large strawberries, chopped
1 orange, peeled and chopped
3 tbsps sugar
3 tbsps lime juice
³/₄ cup cognac
1 bottle champagne

Combine all the ingredients except the champagne in a punch bowl. Cover and let the mixture sit for 1 hour. Pour the champagne, well-chilled, over the fruit. Stir, and pour immediately into chilled glasses.

Index